CUTTING-EDGE SCIENCE

STEM CELLS

By Caroline Green

New
Forest
Press

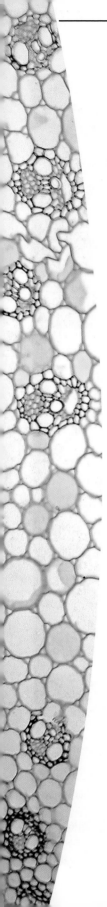

Publisher: Melissa Fairley
Art Director: Faith Booker
Editor: Miranda Smith
Designer: Sara Greasley
Production Controller: Ed Green
Production Manager: Suzy Kelly

ISBN: 978-1-84898-325-0
Library of Congress Control Number: 2010925207
Tracking number: nfp0001

North American edition copyright © *TickTock* Entertainment Ltd. 2010
First published in North America in 2010 by *New Forest Press*,
PO Box 784, Mankato, MN 56002
www.newforestpress.com

Printed in the USA
9 8 7 6 5 4 3 2 1

Picture credits (t=top; b=bottom; c=center; OFC= outside front cover; OBC=outside back cover): Corbis: 49b (Kyunghyang Shinmun/epa). iStock: 17, 24–25, 30t, 32–33, 36–37, 42t, 43b, 52–53t, 60l. Science Photo Library: 5; 6t (Dr. Yorgos Nikas); 9 (Dr. Gopal Murti); 10 (David Mack); 11 (Dr. Gopal Murti); 12t (Edelmann); 13t (Juergen Berger); 14–15bc (Steve Gshmeissner); 15t (Thomas Deerinck, NCMIR); 18t (Steve Gschmeissner); 19t (C. J. Guerin, PhD, MRC Toxicology Unit); 20–21; 23b (Mauro Fermariello); 27b (BSIP, Ducloux); 28t (BSIP, VEM); 29 (Simon Fraser); 34t (Steve Gschmeissner); 35b (Steve Horrell); 37t (Dr. L.Orci, University of Geneva); 39 (Dr. Olivier Schwartz, Institut Pasteur); 40t (Pasieka); 41t (Steve Gschmeissner); 44–45bc (Pasieka); 44t (Hank Morgan); 51t (Deloche); 54b (Philippe Plailly); 55t (Steve Gschmeissner); 57 (Philippe Plailly); 58t (Mauro Fermariello); 59t (James King-Holmes). Shutterstock: OFC; OBC (all); 1 (all and throughout); 2, 3 (all and throughout), 7l, 7c (all and throughout), 22t, 26, 31b, 46t, 47b, 48–49, 50t

Every effort has been made to trace the copyright holders, and we apologize in advance for any omissions. We would be pleased to insert the appropriate acknowledgments in any subsequent edition of this publication.

The author has asserted her right to be identified as the author of this book in accordance with the Copyright, Design, and Patents Act, 1988.
The author and publisher would like to thank Ingrid Heersche at the MRC Centre for Regenerative Medicine, Edinburgh, Scotland, for her help.

NOTE TO READERS
The website addresses are correct at the time of publishing. However, due to the ever-changing nature of the Internet, websites and content may change. Some websites can contain links that are unsuitable for children. The publisher is not responsible for changes in content or website addresses. We advise that Internet searches are supervised by an adult.

CONTENTS

A MEDICAL FRONTIER

HUMANS HAVE BEEN MAKING USE OF NATURE FOR THOUSANDS OF YEARS. THE WORD *BIOTECHNOLOGY* SOUNDS MODERN, BUT IT LITERALLY MEANS ANY BRANCH OF SCIENCE WHERE WHOLE OR PARTS OF LIVING ORGANISMS ARE USED TO CREATE SPECIFIC RESULTS. SO WHEN OUR ANCESTORS USED FUNGI OR YEASTS TO MAKE WINE, BREAD, OR CHEESE, THIS WAS EARLY BIOTECHNOLOGY IN ACTION.

In today's world, the fuller definition of biotechnology is any branch of science in which living cells are used to make or modify products, improve plants or animals, or develop microorganisms for specific purposes. Like all new branches of science, stem cell research has attracted great excitement and controversy. However, it is an area of medical research that holds enormous promise.

WHAT ARE STEM CELLS?

Stem cells are cells that have the potential to develop into many different types of cells in the body. Because of this ability, they may one day help create a type of "repair kit" for the human body. Imagine a world where heart disease could be cured by injecting new healthy heart cells into damaged tissue. Or where people with diabetes could produce **insulin** from new healthy cells in the pancreas Diseases that affect the nervous system, such as Alzheimer's and Parkinson's, may be cured by new brain cells. Or the risky business of developing new drug treatments could be carried out without risk on living tissues grown from stem cells. Developments like these could save or improve the lives of millions of people worldwide and revolutionize the way in which we think about health and disease.

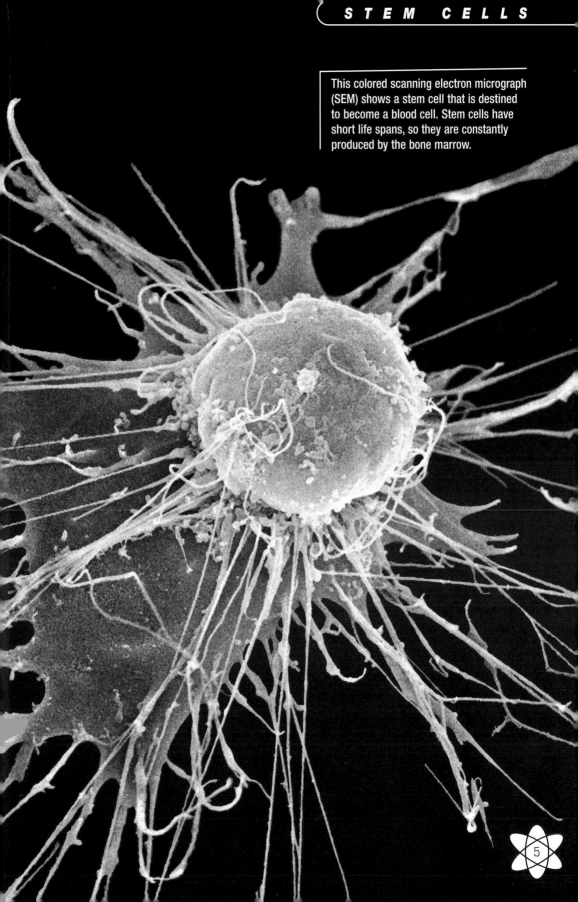

This colored scanning electron micrograph (SEM) shows a stem cell that is destined to become a blood cell. Stem cells have short life spans, so they are constantly produced by the bone marrow.

This is a human embryo six days after fertilization. It is a hollow ball of cells with a fluid center.

AN ETHICAL MINEFIELD

Stem cell research began in the 1960s, but it was not until 1998, when scientists isolated human stem cells, that its true potential was realized. Some experts remain skeptical, but many believe that the potential for stem cell science is huge.

OBSTACLES

When topics such as **cloning** or stem cells come up, there will invariably be two passionate sides to the debate. The controversy with stem cell research lies with the raw materials needed to carry it out. Although stem cells can be grown from adult tissues, by far the most versatile and promising types come from human **embryos** that are only a few days old. These are usually donated to research centers by people having fertility treatment. However, some people believe that it is wrong to carry out any form of research on embryos, whatever the possible ultimate benefits to humankind.

There are also practical obstacles, and genuine treatments are still in the planning stages. However, there are many scientists working around the world who believe the potential of this branch of science is so huge that all of these hurdles can be tackled. As actor and Parkinson's disease sufferer Michael J. Fox said in his autobiography, *Lucky Man*: "If the potential of stem cell research is realized, it would mean an end to the suffering of millions of people. Stem cells could lead to breakthroughs in developing treatments and cures for almost any terminal or catastrophic disease you can think of."

When stem cells are donated by giving blood, the required blood components are separated by an apheresis machine (not seen). The rest of the blood is returned to the donor.

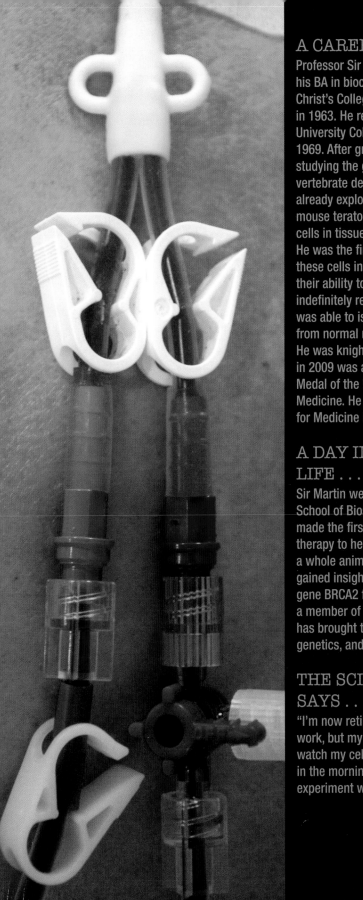

A CAREER IN SCIENCE

Professor Sir Martin Evans obtained his BA in biochemistry from Christ's College, Cambridge, U.K, in 1963. He received a PhD from University College London in 1969. After graduating, he began studying the genetic control of vertebrate development. He had already explored the cultures of mouse teratocarcinoma stem cells in tissue culture systems. He was the first to maintain these cells in conditions where their ability to differentiate was indefinitely retained. In 1981, he was able to isolate similar cells from normal mouse embryos. He was knighted in 2004 and in 2009 was awarded the Gold Medal of the Royal Society of Medicine. He won the Nobel Prize for Medicine in 2007.

A DAY IN THE LIFE . . .

Sir Martin went to Cardiff University's School of Biosciences in 1999 and made the first demonstration of gene therapy to help treat cystic fibrosis in a whole animal. His laboratory has also gained insights into the breast cancer gene BRCA2 function. Now retired, he is a member of the Wales Gene Park, which has brought together life sciences, genetics, and clinical expertise.

THE SCIENTIST SAYS . . .

"I'm now retired from practical scientific work, but my greatest delight was to watch my cells growing and to come in the morning to see how the latest experiment was fairing."

CHAPTER ONE

WHAT IS A CELL?

CELLS ARE THE BASIC BUILDING BLOCKS OF ALL LIFE ON EARTH. A CELL IS THE SMALLEST ORGANISM CAPABLE OF BEING INDEPENDENTLY ALIVE. IT MAY COME AS A SINGLE UNIT—SUCH AS A BACTERIUM— OR IN A COMPLEX GROUP OF 100 TRILLION, SUCH AS THE CELLS THAT MAKE UP A HUMAN BEING.

THE FIRST CELL

In 1665, it was an English scientist, Robert Hooke, who first used the word *cell* when he looked through his basic microscope at a thin sliver of cork. The small holes reminded him of the rooms in a monastery. It was only ten years later that people realized that cells are not empty after all—they are filled with a jellylike substance called cytoplasm.

TYPES OF CELLS

There are two main types of cells: **prokaryotic** and **eukaryotic**. Prokaryotes are one-celled organisms that do not develop or change into more complex forms. Eukaryotic organisms have more than one cell and include everything from the tiniest fungus to all plants, animals, and humans. Eukaryotic cells are complex, have a **nucleus**, and contain various compartments, or structures, that perform specific functions. These compartments are called **organelles**. There are a dozen different types found in eukaryotic cells, including the nucleus, **mitochondria**, and **ribosomes**. The outer lining is known as the **plasma membrane**, and this keeps a cell protected and separate from the environment around it. Each component has its own specialized function. Cells are all individually alive, even if they cannot survive independently. They all contain information—**genes**—that determine who we are.

This section through a mammalian cell show the nucleus (pink), where genes are stored. The dark area (brown) at the center of the nucleus is the most active part of the structure, the nucleolus.

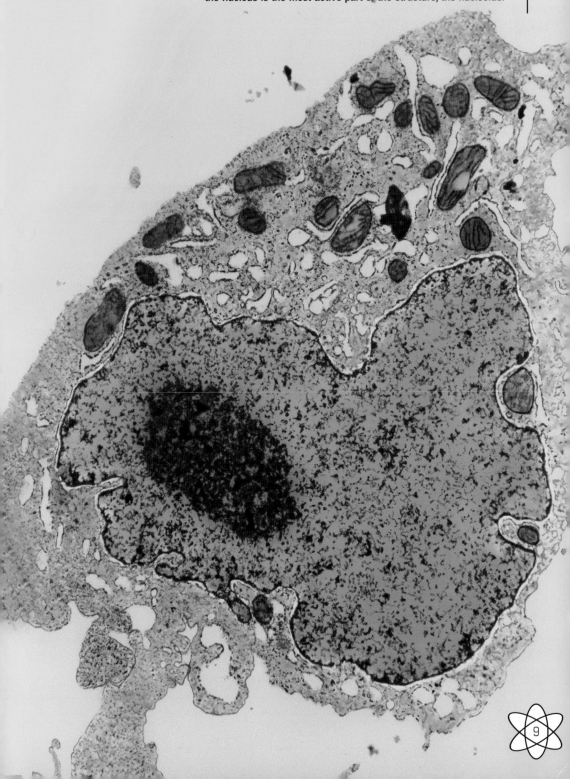

This hollow ball of cells is a blastocyst and is one of the first stages of embryonic development. It is implanting itself into the wall of the mother's uterus (womb), where it will develop into a baby.

WHAT DO CELLS DO?

In the first few hours after a human egg is fertilized, the single cell begins to divide. Within four days, a hollow sphere of cells called a **blastocyst** has formed. The cluster of cells in the middle goes on to form every part of a human body. They produce liver cells for the development of the liver, skin cells for the skin, and so on. There are around 200 different types of cells in our bodies.

To carry out their different functions, cells make a range of proteins. These are large complex **carbohydrates** made from chains of amino acids, and the instructions to make these proteins comes from genes. For example, it is only in cells in the eye that a protein is made that allows us to detect light.

All of the cells in our body are able to recognize one another as belonging to the same body. Viruses, bacteria, and other invaders are identified and trigger the immune system to act.

CELL DEATH

Around 50 million cells in your body will have died and been replaced in the time it takes to read this sentence. There are many different things that can kill a cell, from infections to poisoning to lack of oxygen, but the body also has its own clever way of getting rid of old cells known as **apoptosis**. This is a way of cells triggering their own death—a sort of cell suicide. When apoptosis goes wrong, it results in a range of diseases. Cancer is the reproduction of cells when, and at a rate that, they should not. And it is believed that degenerative diseases such as Alzheimer's and Parkinson's may be a result of cells dying too fast. Scientists also think that the **AIDS** virus exploits this natural process by tricking immune cells into killing themselves.

The white blood cell in the center of this image is undergoing apoptosis, or cell death.

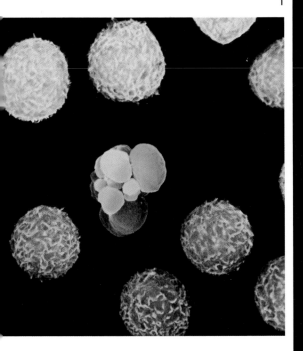

A CAREER IN SCIENCE

Professor Sir Ian Wilmut is the director of the Medical Research Council Centre for Regenerative Medicine at the University of Edinburgh, Scotland. He is also the group leader of cellular reprogramming at the center. His research group works on understanding the mechanisms of pluripotent stem cells in the study of inherited disease. Professor Wilmut worked at the Roslin Institute in Scotland for more than 30 years, where he led the research team that, in 1996, first cloned a mammal—a sheep named Dolly.

A DAY IN THE LIFE . . .

As an early career scientist, Professor Wilmut did a lot of work in the laboratory, but today, he spends most of his time managing the center and his research group, giving lectures, and talking to journalists. He sometimes travels at home and overseas for conferences or to develop future collaborations with partner institutes.

THE SCIENTIST SAYS . . .

"I want to learn something new every day and find it very rewarding to develop new ideas and insights together with my colleagues. I believe that research on stem cells will make a huge contribution to medicine over the next 50 years. Stem cell research is very exciting, and I think researchers should be more ambitious to use their insights to discover drugs and develop cell and gene therapies."

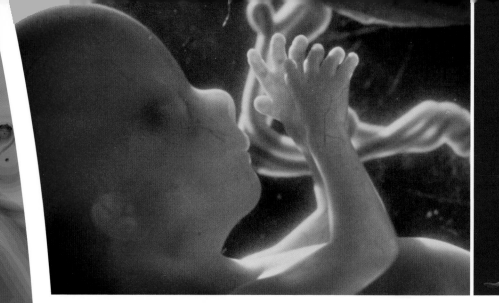

This fetus is four months old. Stem cells can be found in the umbilical cord that joins the fetus to its mother's placenta, and the cord supplies it with oxygenated, nutrient-rich blood.

WHAT ARE STEM CELLS?

Unlike cells that have a role destined for them, stem cells have the ability to develop into any of the cells in the human body.

Stem cells are formed in the earliest days of life. First, there is a single cell created by a fertilized egg—a **zygote**. This is described as **totipotent**, which means that it has the "total potential" to give rise to all of the different cells in the body. This cell splits into two, then four, then eight, and so on, eventually leading to trillions.

Around five days after conception, a blastocyst smaller than a grain of sand is formed, with around 150 cells. This contains two types of cells. The **trophoblast**, or outer cell, will eventually become the placenta, which carries food and oxygen from the mother to the developing fetus. The inner part is known as the **inner cell mass (ICM)**, and this contains all of the cells that will make up the human body. These are known as **pluripotent**, meaning that can create plural, or many, cells.

At this stage, the ICM cells have the capability to become any part of a human body. Within three weeks, the cells will have differentiated and started to take on various roles. Pre-epithelial, or prenervous system, cells

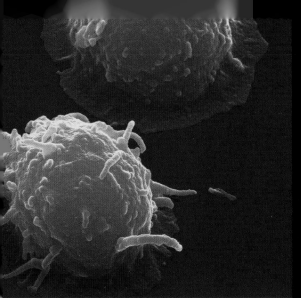

These two stem cells, taken from umbilical cord blood, could become any part of the human body.

A CAREER IN SCIENCE

Born in Hong Kong and educated at National Taiwan University in Taiwan, Dr. Anthony Chan graduated from the University of Wisconsin-Madison. At the Oregon National Primate Research Center, he worked on developing the world's first transgenic monkey. He joined the Yerkes National Primate Research Center at Emory University, Georgia, to create the first transgenic monkey model of Huntington's disease. He is now an assistant professor in the Department of Human Genetics at Emory University School of Medicine.

will have developed, along with premuscle and connective tissue cells and preinternal organ cells. These early stem cells are known as **embryonic stem cells**.

Even when the body has fully formed, some parts, such as the bone marrow, muscles, and brain, continue to make replacement cells for those lost through injury, disease, or just wear and tear. These are known as adult stem cells, although children have them, too. Stem cells can also be found in the umbilical cord that joins a baby to its mother's placenta. Other potential sources discovered in recent times include the actual placenta, the fallopian tubes, and a type of blood cell called a myoendothelial cell.

A DAY IN THE LIFE . . .

Dr. Chan's team focuses on investigating the transgenic primate model of human diseases such as Huntington's disease. In addition, they have been able to grow stem cells from monkey dental pulp—the central part of a tooth that contains soft tissue.

THE SCIENTIST SAYS . . .

"One of the most satisfying experiences is when I receive appreciation from individuals of our work, which may one day be able to help their family or loved one. I hope to use my expertise to develop a model that will help us advance our knowledge in human diseases and educate the general public to understand the importance of a model system in finding cures."

A SHORT HISTORY

It was in the mid-1800s that scientists realized that cells are the basic building blocks of life. In the early 1900s, it was discovered that a type of cell in the bone marrow and bloodstream (a **hematopoietic**, or blood-forming, stem cell) is able to create new blood cells. Scientists realized that cells are capable of regenerating and producing new versions of themselves.

The idea that medicine could develop treatments using new healthy cells to replace diseased or dead ones made a huge leap forward in the 1950s when doctors carried out the first successful bone marrow transplant in someone suffering from leukemia.

Then, in 1981, a young researcher named Gail Martin in the United States isolated mouse embryonic cells that were the precursors to all other growth. She named them "stem" cells, because the development of the creature "stemmed" from these early cells.

CELL LINES

In 1998, James Thompson from the University of Wisconsin-Madison isolated human cells from the ICM and developed the first embryonic **cell lines**. This was a real breakthrough, and the implications became hot topics in the media. Cell lines are a crucial tool in stem cell research. The term describes cells that have been grown in a laboratory so that they replicate indefinitely, producing identical copies of themselves. Today, there are many more animal embryonic stem cell lines than there are human in different projects around the world.

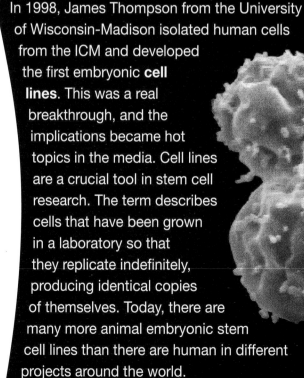

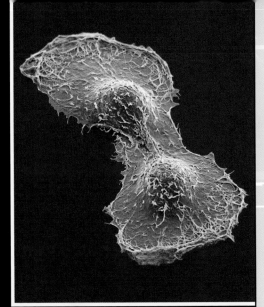

This cell is undergoing the final stage of cell division to produce two daughter nuclei. It is a cultured cancer cell that is widely used in biological and medical reserach.

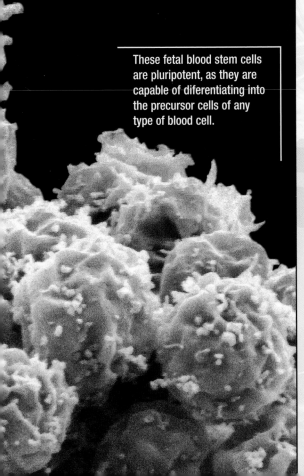

These fetal blood stem cells are pluripotent, as they are capable of diferentiating into the precursor cells of any type of blood cell.

INVESTIGATING THE EVIDENCE: LIPOSUCTION AND STEM CELLS

The investigation: Scientists wanted to establish whether the fat tissue left over from cosmetic surgery procedures such as liposuction could be induced to become a viable source of pluripotent stem cells.

The scientists: Dr. Michael Longaker and Dr. Joseph Wu from Stanford University's Institute for Stem Cell Biology and Regenerative Medicine in Palo Alto, California.

Collecting the evidence: The team studied fat cells known as **adipose-**derived stromal (connective tissue) and skin-derived cells, which are multipotent. They are renewable, abundant, and are removed during cosmetic surgery procedures such as liposuction. The team injected viruses into these cells and introduced genes that reprogrammed them to grow differently.

The conclusion: The cells were successfully prompted to pluripotency, and the process was around twice as fast and 20 times more efficient than using fibroblasts or skin cells, which are grown in a lab for three weeks before they can be reprogrammed. The fat cells were able to be used right away. The team believes that these cells could be a useful and plentiful resource for future work.

CHAPTER TWO

NEW TREATMENTS

THE POSSIBLE TREATMENTS THAT STEM CELLS MAY ONE DAY OFFER COULD AFFECT MILLIONS OF PEOPLE. IT SOUNDS LIKE A FAIRY TALE, KEEPING US FOREVER YOUNG AND HEALTHY. BUT FOR MANY MILLIONS OF PEOPLE, REPLACING DAMAGED OR DISEASED CELLS WITH HEALTHY NORMAL ONES COULD BE A MATTER OF LIFE AND DEATH.

STATE OF PLAY

There are very few real stem cell treatments in practice. The most well established is the use of bone marrow cells, which are injected to treat leukemia. Unfortunately, there are many clinics around the world offering dangerous or ineffective treatments directly to the public.

By contrast, there are exciting possibilities coming out of work done by reputable scientists. There are certain conditions and diseases that are discussed most often in terms of their possible benefits. Degenerative diseases of the brain and nervous system, such as Parkinson's disease and multiple sclerosis (MS), are currently incurable. However, research is being carried out into how stem cell science may one day prevent these diseases. Strokes and spinal cord injuries that leave people paralyzed may also be cured. Diabetes, which the World Health Organization (WHO) says is now reaching epidemic proportions, could be wiped out by replacing the diseased tissues of the pancreas with new healthy tissues. Other uses could include the repair of heart tissue damaged by cardiovascular disease and heart attacks, as well as curing diseases that involve the immune system, such as arthritis.

Possible future uses of cultured stem cells could include treatments for cancer.

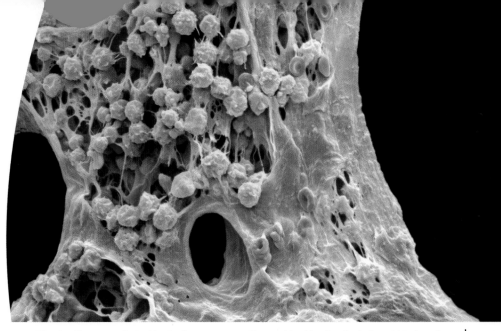

Blood cells are made inside the bone marrow. Here, white blood cells (colored blue) and red blood cells are shown in the connective tissue framework of the bone marrow.

WHERE DO STEM CELLS COME FROM?

In order to carry out their research, scientists need to establish what are known as stem cell lines. These are populations of cells that replicate themselves over and over again in vitro (in a laboratory). To do this, the scientists need stem cells.

CURRENT RESEARCH

Embryonic stem cells of the pluripotent variety come from ICMs of embryos that are only a few days old. The majority used in research have come from spare embryos donated by couples having fertility treatment. Stem cells are also found in many of the tissues of the human body. They are undifferentiated, which means that they have not yet become a particular type of cell, and their role is to help repair and look after the tissues in which they are found. They are described as **multipotent**, which is not as versatile as pluripotent, but they can develop into a range of cells that are closely related. Hematopoietic stem cells, which are found mostly in the bone marrow, can develop into the red blood cells, white blood cells, and platelets that constitute blood.

▶▶ http://stemcells.nih.gov

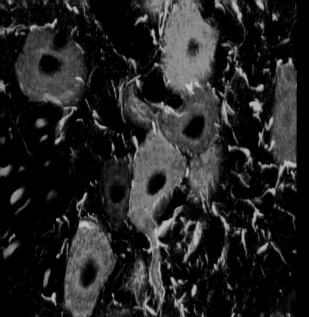

Nerve cells (red) in the brain stem control automatic functions such as breathing.

OTHER SOURCES

Stem cells can be taken from the umbilical cords of newborn babies. These are a rich source of stem cells that can turn into cells in the blood and immune system. When a baby is born, parents can opt to store cord blood for any future treatment needed by the baby, other members of the family, or even strangers. Adult stem cells have been identified in organs and tissues including the brain, heart, blood and blood vessels, skeletal muscle, placenta, skin, teeth, heart, gut, liver, ovaries, and testes. Sources from adults and byproducts of birth are popular because they get around the ethical hurdles that embryonic stem cells present.

A CAREER IN SCIENCE

Dr. Stephen Minger is the director of the Stem Cell Biology Laboratory and a senior lecturer at the new Wolfson Centre for Age-related Diseases at King's College London, U.K. Over the past 15 years, his stem cell research team has worked with stem cell populations, as well as mouse and human embryonic stem (ES) cells. In 2002, with Dr. Susan Pickering and Professor Peter Braude, Dr. Minger was awarded one of the first two licenses granted by the U.K. Human Fertilization and Embryology Authority (HEFA) for the derivation of human ES cells. His team generated the first human embryonic stem cell line in the U.K. and was one of the first groups to deposit this into the U.K. Stem Cell Bank.

A DAY IN THE LIFE . . .

A typical day for Dr. Minger involves assessing new technology that may be important to his team's research, evaluating the data that the team is generating, and spending many hours in meetings and international conference calls with members of his extended research group and collaborators.

THE SCIENTIST SAYS . . .

"The most challenging aspect of our stem cell work is how we translate this amazing technology to real clinical applications."

These fat cells (blue), also known as adipocytes or lipocytes, are found in bone marrow tissue. They store energy as an insulating layer of fat.

INDUCED PLURIPOTENT STEM CELLS

Embryonic stem cells (ESCs) are the most versatile in terms of potential **therapeutic** uses. But what if adult stem cells, which have none of the ethical considerations of ESCs, could be made to behave like ESCs? That is the thinking behind the development of **induced pluripotent stem (iPS) cells**.

Adult stem cells have the ability to be pluripotent, and it is possible to "turn on" this pluripotency by genetically reprogramming the cells. The first breakthrough came in 2008 when scientists Shinya Yamanaka and Kazutoshi Takahashi of Kyoto University in Japan created iPS cells from mice. The following year, the same process was carried out with human adult stem cells.

CHALLENGES FOR THE FUTURE

This was a huge advance, but it did not translate into treatments for real patients. These iPS cells carry a high risk of becoming cancerous, and it would be too dangerous to use them in human trials. However, it could be the first step on a journey that ends with treatments, especially as scientists from the Scripps Research Institute in La Jolla, California, discovered in April 2009 that it is possible to trigger this process in a safer way, bypassing the genetic

▶▶ http://en.wikipedia.org/wiki/Induced_pluripotent_stem_cell

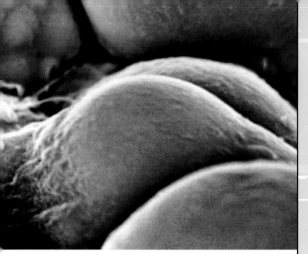

reprogramming and using proteins instead. So far, this technique is not quite as effective as using genes. However, changes take place in this area so quickly that it is possible that great strides will have been made even as this book is being printed.

Despite the fact that iPS cells are not in use for treatments, they are extremely useful in helping scientists study diseases, and they provide a good alternative to animal testing.

SOURCES OF CELLS

Scrapings of human skin from volunteers are the usual source of cells to create iPS cells. Many other potential sources, including cells taken from the liver and stomach, are being investigated around the world. One team is studying the potential of fat cells to create iPS cells.

INVESTIGATING THE EVIDENCE: GENERATING IPS CELLS

The investigation: Scientists wanted to generate induced pluripotent stem (iPS) cells without permanent genetic modifications and without using viruses.

The scientists: Dr. Keisuke Kaji, MRC Centre for Regenerative Medicine, University of Edinburgh, U.K., and Professor Andras Nagy and Dr. Knut Woltjen, Samuel Lunenfeld Research Institute, Mount Sinai Hospital, Toronto, Canada.

Collecting the evidence: Four reprogramming genes were put into a delivery system called a transposon. This is a mobile sequence of **DNA** that can move to different positions within a genome or be excised (taken away) from it. It allows for the introduction and removal of genes from outside the organism without altering the sequence of the genome.

The conclusion: The team proved the iPS cells derived with the nonviral system are genuinely pluripotent. It was also confirmed that the removal of exogenous genes was very precise, and in more than 95 percent of the cases, the iPS cells had no mutations. This is currently one of the safest ways to generate human iPS cells without genetic modifications.

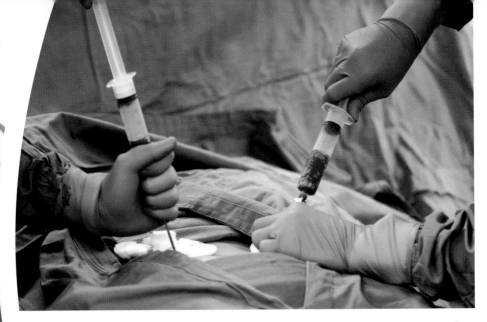

Bone marrow plays a key role in blood production. Here, healthy bone marrow stem cells are being harvested from a donor for transplantation into another patient.

CURRENT TREATMENTS

Thousands of people around the world have been saved by donated bone marrow, the most well-established therapy in the world that relies on the use of stem cells. When someone has a disease such as leukemia or lymphoma, it is often necessary to give very high doses of chemotherapy and radiation. These treatments destroy many cells in the body and particularly target those that divide rapidly, a characteristic of cancer cells.

Bone marrow is the spongy tissue inside bones where the various types of blood cells are produced, including the white cells that are a crucial part of our immune system. Stem cells—haematopoietic cells—are responsible for this, and they are easily wiped out by chemotherapy and radiation.

There are two procedures that can help restore these stem cells. In 1968, the first successful bone marrow transplantation (BMT) was carried out. Today, PBSCT (peripheral blood stem cell transplantation) uses stem cells that have been found in the bloodstream. For PBSCT, there are three possible procedures:

- autologous—where a patient receives their own stem cells,

▶▶ http://hcd2.bupa.co.uk/fact_sheets/html/Bone_marrow.html

harvested before a cancer treatment begins

- syngeneic—where a transplant is received from an identical twin
- allogeneic—where a patient receives stem cells from their brother, sister, or parent—or a donor where there is a match

Another common use of stem cells is in skin grafts for treating patients with severe burns. A small amount of unburned skin is taken, and stem cells are isolated. These are used to grow new skin. This treatment has been in use for 25 years and has saved many lives.

This epidermal strip has been grown from epidermal cells in a laboratory.

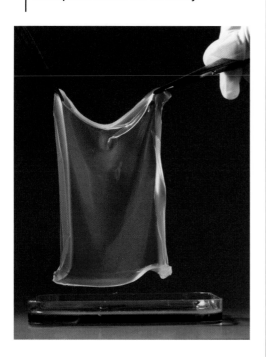

INVESTIGATING THE EVIDENCE: BONE MARROW CELLS

The investigation: Bone marrow transplantation is used to treat patients suffering from blood cancers. The team investigated whether bone marrow cells fuse with the recipient's cells after transplantation.

The scientists: Professor Nicholas Zavazava, Sabrina Bonde, and Ryan Stultz, University of Iowa, and Mehrdad Pedram, assistant professor, University of Tehran, Iran.

Collecting the evidence: The team used mice with a reporter gene, which helps identify cells of interest. When bone marrow cells from two mice strains were fused, the reporter gene was activated. This method was used to investigate cell fusion in a mouse after bone marrow transplantation.

The conclusion: The team found that bone marrow cell types formed fused cells that appeared larger in size than nonfused cells. Not only did the donor cells fuse with bone marrow cells but also with cells of the heart, kidney, liver, and gut. The results implied that cell fusion might be a way in which bone marrow cells repair damaged tissues inside our bodies. Hybrid cells could potentially be generated to help prevent rejection of transplanted bone marrow cells.

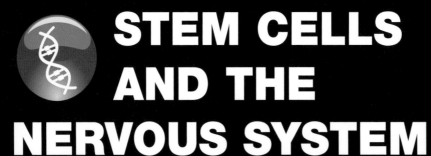

CHAPTER THREE

STEM CELLS AND THE NERVOUS SYSTEM

YOUR NERVOUS SYSTEM IS MORE COMPLEX AND SOPHISTICATED THAN ANY COMPUTER THAT HAS EVER BEEN INVENTED. IT IS THE CONTROL CENTER FOR EVERYTHING YOU FEEL, THINK, AND DO. WHETHER YOU ARE LAUGHING AT A JOKE, RUNNING TO CATCH THE BUS, EATING YOUR LUNCH, OR PLAYING A VIDEO GAME, ALL OF YOUR RESPONSES RELY ON THIS NETWORK OF CELLS.

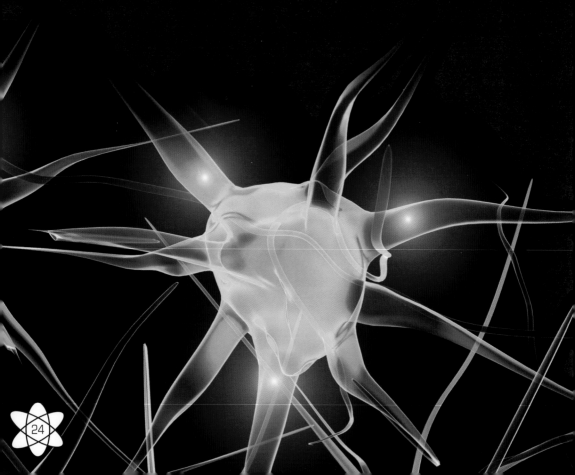

The nervous system is made up of your brain, spinal cord, and a range of specialized nerve cells called **neurons**. It is usually divided into the central nervous system (CNS) and the peripheral nervous system (PNS). The CNS is the brain and spinal cord, the column of tissue that travels from the base of the skull down the back and that has nerves branching off to all parts of the body. The PNS is all of the other nerves that connect the CNS to the rest of the body.

THE ROLE OF NEURONS

Neurons carry messages throughout the body by a mixture of chemical and electrical means. Our bodies contain a truly staggering number of neurons. A human brain alone is likely to contain around 100 billion that, if laid end to end, would stretch for around 620 mi. (1,000km). They may vary drastically in size—the smallest are only four microns long (1,000 microns equals one millimeter), and the longest are up to 3.3 ft. (1m) in length.

There are three main types of neurons: sensory, motor, and association. Sensory neurons send impulses between the spinal cord and the sense organs, such as the eyes, ears, nose, and mouth. These are responsible for your ability to smell a baking cake, watch it emerge from the oven, and enjoy the taste once it is cool enough to eat. Motor neurons transfer the impulses to and from the muscles and glands of the body in response to various stimuli. When you speak, walk, swallow, or pull back from a hot radiator, your motor neurons are in charge. Finally, association neurons, found in the brain and spinal cord, connect the motor neurons and the sensory neurons.

Until relatively recently, it was believed that neurons did not have the ability to renew themselves. However, in the last ten years there have been great leaps in our understanding, and we now know that neurons are able to regenerate. This has exciting implications for future treatments.

DISEASES OF THE NERVOUS SYSTEM

There are several diseases that attack the cells of the nervous system. Motor neuron disease (MND) and Parkinson's disease are two of the most well known, and they are both devastating.

MOTOR NEURONE DISEASE

MND refers to a group of diseases that attack the motor neurones—the cells that control voluntary muscle activities such as walking, speaking, swallowing, and breathing. Over time, this causes a wasting away and weakening of the muscles, combined with rigidity. There are different types of MND, including amyothrophic lateral sclerosis (ALS), also known as Lou Gehrig's disease after a famous American baseball player. The condition eventually leads to death because the muscles that control

English scientist Stephen Hawking is one of the most famous sufferers of ALS.

breathing no longer work. The disease usually affects people over the age of 50, and men are more likely to get it than women. The cause of MND is not completely understood, nor is there any cure to date.

PARKINSON'S DISEASE

An English physician named James Parkinson wrote a pamphlet in 1817 entitled "An Essay on the Shaking Palsy." Forty years later, other symptoms were added to the list, and the disease became known as Parkinson's. It now affects around one

▶▶ http://quest.nasa.gov/neuron/background/nervsys.html

in 500 people over the age of 60, although it can occasionally affect people in their 40s or younger. Symptoms usually start on just one side of the body, including weakness or tremors. Although it is not life threatening, people with Parkinson's may become depressed or develop other conditions because they are unable to function normally.

This disease is caused by imbalances in the brain between two chemicals—dopamine and acetylcholine. These usually work together to transmit messages between the cells of the nerves and muscles, and they help us coordinate our movements. Parkinson's occurs when the cells that produce dopamine are lost, but it is not known why this happens. There is no cure.

Parkinson's disease is caused by the loss of nerve cells from the basal ganglia (dark blue areas in the box), which results in a lack of dopamine.

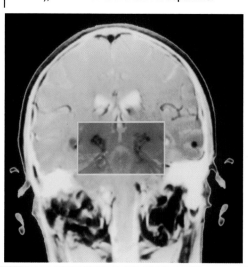

INVESTIGATING THE EVIDENCE: MODELS FOR DISEASES

The investigation: The ability to derive iPS cells directly from human skin cells and generate any cell type in a petri dish offers a unique opportunity to study human diseases and develop models of them.

The scientists: Shinya Yamanaka, Kyoto University, Japan, together with Rudolf Jaenisch, Whitehead Institute for Biomedical Research, Massachusetts, James Thompson, University of Wisconsin, Austin Smith, University of Cambridge, U.K., and Douglas Melton, Harvard University, Massachusetts.

Collecting the evidence: The team routinely obtains skin samples and ES cell genes from which they get patient-specific iPS cells. These are maintained in special equipment to grow human ES and iPS cells. The cells are used for differentiation in order to obtain different somatic cells. The scientists constantly use different materials and growth factors to obtain cells at higher efficiencies and purities.

The conclusion: The group has been able to generate iPS cells from skin biopsies of patients with different diseases, including Parkinson's. This has given them an unprecedented opportunity to test the differences between healthy donor and patient-derived neuron cells in a variety of experimental tests.

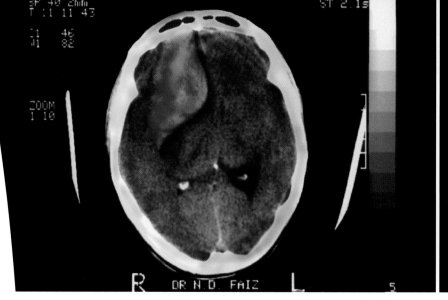

Here, a bleed, or hemorrhagic stroke (red, left), has occurred in the brain. This is a dangerous condition that puts pressure on the brain.

NERVOUS SYSTEM DAMAGE

Damage to the nervous system can happen in an accident or from sudden events such as a stroke, as well as from disease. Because most of the cells in the nervous system cannot regrow, these events may be devastating for those who suffer them. Spinal cord injuries do not usually cut the spinal cord, but they may cause the vertebrae to break or be compressed, which may in turn crush or destroy the axons. These nerve cell extensions carry signals up and down the spinal column from the brain to the rest of the body. Some or almost all of the axons may be affected, so there may be eventual recovery in some cases and complete paralysis in others. There can be a range of other health issues, including fatal heart and lung problems.

Spinal cord injuries are usually permanent, but it may be possible through physical rehabilitation and drug therapies to recover some movement or sensation over time. However, for people who are quadriplegic, where all movement and function in the four limbs are lost, it is unlikely that they will recover their use.

Brain trauma may also be permanent. This can happen if there has been a serious head injury or if the blood supply has been cut

▶▶ www.apparelyzed.com/spinalcord.html

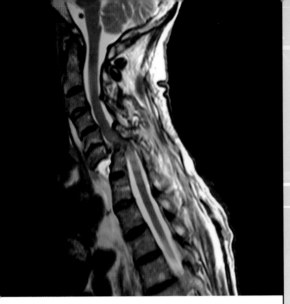

The spinal column here has fractured in an accident and is compressing the spinal cord (red).

off. And a stroke is another potentially devastating event that affects the nervous system. It is described as a "brain attack" and happens when the blood supply that feeds the brain's cells with nutrients and oxygen is cut off. This may happen because of a blockage—an **ischaemic stroke**— caused by a blood clot, or a bleed— a **hemorrhagic stroke**. This occurs when a blood vessel in the brain bursts. In the developed world, stroke is the third leading cause of death after heart disease and cancer. In fact, stroke causes the most disability of any chronic disease. Not smoking, eating a healthy, balanced diet, and doing regular exercise are the best ways to prevent a stroke from occurring.

INVESTIGATING THE EVIDENCE: STROKES AND STEM CELLS

The investigation: A team at the University of Texas Medical School wanted to know if it is safe to give a stroke patient intravenous injections of his or her own bone marrow cells in order to clear the way for study of how these cells can enhance recovery after a stroke.

The scientists: Dr. Sean Savitz, an associate professor of neurology at the university's medical school, led the study with a team of collaborators.

Collecting the evidence: Cells were harvested from the bone marrow from the leg of a male stroke victim. The cells were injected into a vein in his arm several hours later. Because they were his own cells, there were no problems with rejection. He had arrived at the hospital unable to speak and with significant weakness on his right side. When he went home two weeks later, he was able to walk, climb stairs unassisted, and his speaking had improved. However, it is unknown if his improvement was due to the cells or to natural recovery.

The conclusion: The study was a first step toward finding out if the procedure is safe. Once this is established, the team will be able to explore the possible benefits.

The vast majority of stem cell treatment trials are carried out using mice and rats in a laboratory—very few trials so far have involved human beings.

THE ROLE OF STEM CELLS

In the future, stem cell science may hold great promise for treating disease of, or injuries to, the nervous system. Until recently, it was believed that nerve cells in the brain and spinal column could not regenerate, but in 2002, scientists discovered that neural stem cells, taken from the brains of adult rats, could mature into functional nerve cells. There have been many recent promising studies that have looked at potential treatments based on this for a range of conditions. One at the University of California suggested that stem cell treatments could help reverse the effects of memory loss. The majority of these trials have used animals and have shown results only in rats and mice.

FIRST EXPERIMENTS

In the summer of 2009, there was a very important breakthrough. A team of pediatricians and stem cell scientists announced that the first human trials using neural stem cells had been successful. The work was carried out at the Oregon Health and Science University Doernbecher Children's Hospital on six children with a rare and fatal condition called Batten disease. The children were given injections of purified neural brain cells directly into the brain and then a year of treatment to stop their bodies from rejecting the foreign tissues. The main purpose of the trial at this early stage was to see whether the stem cells could be tolerated by human patients, and in this respect the experiment has been successful.

Elsewhere, the first-ever clinical trial using stem cells to repair spinal cord injuries in humans is now taking place. A company in California has been given the official go-ahead. It is still early days in trials where stem cells are being studied as possible cures for neurodegenerative diseases, but the building blocks are in place and advances are happening all the time.

Although the Batten disease trial was not intended to produce major therapeutic benefits, it gives hope for the future.

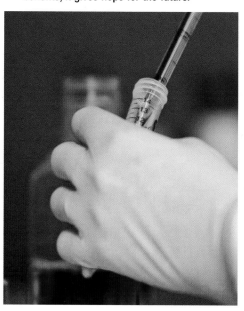

A CAREER IN SCIENCE

Dr. Stephen Huhn is the head of the Central Nervous System Program at StemCells, Inc. in the United States. He directs the company's preclinical and clinical development programs and is on leave from Stanford University School of Medicine, California, where he is an associate professor of neurosurgery and the chief of ppediatric neurosurgery.

A DAY IN THE LIFE OF . . .

Dr. Huhn's work involves coordinating basic science and clinical research for StemCells, Inc., and focusing on developing stem cells for the potential treatment of a variety of central nervous system disorders. A typical day is spent interacting with scientists and clinicians at universities, regulatory agencies, and ethics committees, with the goal of advancing stem cell research and conducting clinical trials.

THE SCIENTIST SAYS . . .

"The most satisfying thing about my work is learning more about the central nervous system and the potential for stem cell therapy. In my current role, I have the opportunity to work in a setting in which we might impact an entire disease, versus my prior role in clinical medicine where the focus was on treating one patient at a time. I hope to contribute significantly in advancing a new way to treat human disease for the benefit of patients suffering from disorders for which there are no treatment options today."

CHAPTER FOUR

THE SILENT KILLER

WE HAVE KNOWN ABOUT DIABETES FOR 3,500 YEARS. IT CURRENTLY AFFECTS 194 MILLION PEOPLE WORLDWIDE AND IS ON THE RISE. BY 2025, THIS FIGURE IS SET TO JUMP TO 472 MILLION. DIABETES IS SOMETIMES CALLED THE "SILENT KILLER" BECAUSE THE SYMPTOMS MAY NOT BE OBVIOUS UNTIL THE DISEASE HAS PROGRESSED QUITE FAR.

WHAT IS DIABETES?

Just as a car needs gas, our bodies require energy each day in order to function properly. How that energy is processed in our bodies is all down to our metabolism. Diabetes occurs when this process is not happening as it should and there is too much sugar in the blood. Most of the food we eat gets broken down into glucose, a type of blood sugar. In order to get to all of the cells where it is needed, glucose is helped along the way by a hormone called insulin. This is produced by a large gland located near the stomach known as the pancreas. If your body does not make enough insulin, or if it does not

Worryingly, doctors are reporting that they are treating more and more young people who are suffering from type two diabetes because of poor diet and lack of exercise.

work in the way in which it should, the glucose cannot reach the cells and remains in the bloodstream. Here, it builds up and is passed out into the urine, without giving the body's cells the energy they require. This leads to diabetes and, over time, can cause serious problems with other organs, such as the eyes, kidneys, nerves, and heart. It can also lead to the necessity for the amputation of limbs.

Prediabetes occurs when the blood sugar is too high but not high enough for a diagnosis of diabetes. It can be the precursor to real diabetes. It may greatly increase the risk of cardiovascular problems, such as heart disease and stroke, but it can be effectively treated by weight loss and exercise.

Diabetes has three different forms, known as type one, type two, and gestational diabetes. Type one is usually found in children, teenagers, and young adults. It accounts for 5–10 percent of diagnoses. It is caused by the body's immune system killing all of the insulin-making cells of the pancreas so that organ can no longer process glucose.

Type two is also known as adult-onset diabetes, but it can happen at any age. Here, the pancreas can make some insulin but not enough. Type two can be brought on by not getting enough exercise and not eating a healthy diet. Gestational diabetes affects pregnant women. Although it disappears after the baby is born, it may cause health complications and lead to an increased risk of type two diabetes in later life.

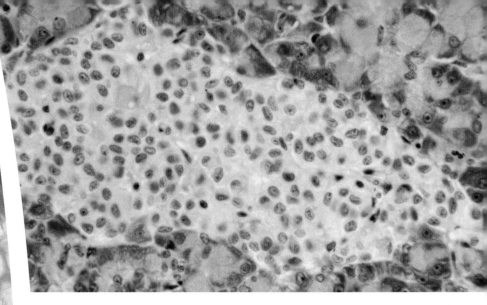

This is a section through an islet of Langerhans in the pancreas. The cells in the islet (yellow) produce the hormones glucagon and insulin, which control blood sugar.

THE ROLE OF THE PANCREAS

We all have a variety of different glands in our bodies, from the pea-size pineal gland near the center of our brains to the largest gland in the body, the pancreas. These glands are part of the endocrine system, which plays a crucial role in most of the functions of the body.

The pancreas is an organ that looks like a banana that has been squashed a little. It is slightly curved and is around the same length and shape. It lies close to the duodenum, the first part of the small intestine, which is connected to the stomach. The pancreas has two main functions: to produce hormones such as insulin and to produce digestive **enzymes**, which help the body break down food once we have eaten it.

This digestive part makes up the vast majority of the pancreas, and the endocrine part (which makes hormones) is only five percent of the cells. These cells are clustered in small groups and scattered throughout the pancreas—they look a little like tiny islands, which is why they have been given the name **pancreatic islet cells**. They are also called islets of Langerhans after a German doctor, Paul Langerhans, who discovered them in 1869.

TYPES OF ISLETS

There are three types: alpha, which produce a hormone called glucagon; beta, which produce insulin; and delta, which produce a hormone called somatostatin. The islets are surrounded by blood vessels, and the hormones they create, such as insulin and glucagon, can get straight into the bloodstream.

If these cells are damaged or killed, they are directly responsible for a person having type one diabetes. For this reason, since the late 1970s, scientists have been carrying out transplants of healthy islet cells into diabetes sufferers. The cells have typically come from donors who have been pronounced brain dead.

This is a lancet, which is used to obtain a drop of blood for a blood sugar test. A separate blood sugar level tester is applied to the resulting blood.

INVESTIGATING THE EVIDENCE: SELF-TESTING FOR DIABETES

The investigation: The goal is to find a simple, painless self-test for diabetes using urine or saliva to help in early diagnosis.

The scientists: Professor Srinivasa R. Nagalla, DiabetOmics LLC, Oregon; Professor Rao Paturi, Nizam's Institute of Medical Sciences, Hyderabad, India; Professor Charles T. Roberts, Jr., Oregon Health and Science University.

Collecting the evidence: The team collected white blood cells from serum, urine, and saliva from people with prediabetes, diabetes, and diabetes with kidney disease. They analyzed the cells to identify particular proteins that are unique to diabetes, using techniques such as electrophoretic gels.

The conclusion: The team has discovered around 100 proteins in urine and saliva that are either higher or lower compared to those in nondiabetics. This has helped them develop tests for proteins using urine or saliva instead of blood. The tests are painless and easy to do without laboratory support, and they provide targeted information.

TREATING DIABETES

People with type one diabetes need to have injections of insulin every day and keep a very careful eye on their blood sugar levels to avoid both falling into a coma or suffering long-term organ damage. So far, the only options are a transplant of the whole pancreas or a transplant of islet cells. However, there are not enough donors, and people may be on waiting lists for a long time. In either case, a patient must take powerful drugs for the rest of their lives to prevent their immune system from rejecting the organ. Their natural immunity is constantly suppressed, leaving them vulnerable to infections.

DIABETES AND STEM CELLS

Beta cells, those precious producers of insulin, develop from stem cells in an embryo by a careful process that is monitored by various genes. One of the main challenges in making beta cells from stem cells is that it is not precisely known where new islet cells come from after birth and into adulthood. Some scientists believe they come from the pancreas, either from ducts there or the islet cells themselves, while others believe they may come from stem cells in the blood. It is still not clear whether stem cells would have to develop into just beta cells or other types of islet cells. Some studies have shown that when beta cells are cultured on their own, they do not work as well as those that are in clusters with other types, as they are found in the body.

There are several different hurdles to be jumped before stem cells will be able to offer real treatments for people suffering from diabetes. But there are many exciting research projects around the world working on doing just that.

Diabetic patients have to give themselves injections of insulin every day. Here, a NovoPen equipped with a portable cartridge measures the correct dosage.

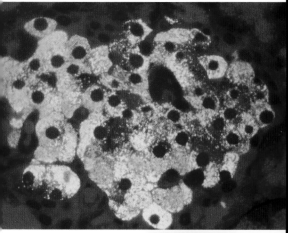

This photograph shows beta cells (dark red circles) clustered in the islets of Langerhans inside the pancreas.

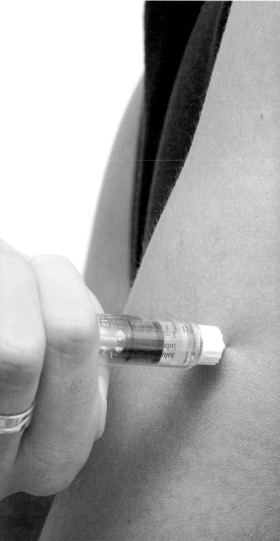

A CAREER IN SCIENCE

Dr. Karen Cosgrove works in the Faculty of Life Sciences at the University of Manchester, U.K. Following postdoctoratal work, she researched diabetes at the University of Sheffield. She has an independent research fellowship at the University of Manchester and runs a small research group looking at new ways to treat diabetes, including using embryonic stem cells to make new pancreatic cells.

A DAY IN THE LIFE OF . . .

Dr. Cosgrove says that there is no such thing as a typical day and that every day is different. She may be writing papers or bidding for grants or going to other lectures to get ideas that boost her own research. She spends time keeping up to date with current research online and then works in the laboratory, checking on how the stem cells are growing and seeing that everything is running smoothly.

THE SCIENTIST SAYS . . .

"The most satisfying parts of my job include getting my research accepted for publication, being awarded funding to carry out more experiments, being invited to talk to other scientists and members of the public about my research, and seeing my students reach their potential at the end of their degree. There is always something to look forward to or a new challenge to tackle."

CHAPTER FIVE

IMMUNITY AND DISEASE

YOUR IMMUNE SYSTEM IS AN INCREDIBLE DEFENSE FORCE THAT WORKS FOR YOU ALL THE TIME. IF YOU THINK OF YOUR BODY AS A COUNTRY, YOU ARE ONE THAT IS CONSTANTLY UNDER THREAT OF INVASION, BOMBARDED BY BACTERIA, VIRUSES, POISONS, AND PARASITES EVERY SINGLE DAY.

LINE OF DEFENSE

The immune system has its own circulation, organs, and highly specialized cells. Lymphatic vessels and lymph nodes are a circulatory system like the blood, but they carry a clear fluid known as **lymph**. This fluid carries important cells— **lymphocytes**—to all of the tissues of the body, where they act as guards against foreign invaders. When we injure ourselves or come into contact with unfriendly microbes, they work to repair damage and repel germs.

Sometimes, the immune system turns upon itself, identifying the body's own tissues as a threat and attacking them as an enemy invader. When this happens, it can cause what is known as an **autoimmune disease** such as rheumatoid arthritis or lupus.

There are currently no cures for these diseases, and sufferers have to find ways to cope using drugs and other therapies.

STEM CELL HELP

A new type of stem cell therapy offers some hope. A patient is given drugs that stimulate the growth of many new hematopoetic cells. He or she then has some blood taken from them, and the stem cells are harvested and frozen. Patients are given large doses of drugs and sometimes radiation during this process. The harvested stem cells are put back into the patient, the idea being that the immune system is kick-started to work properly. The procedure has a high failure rate and is risky, but it can be effective.

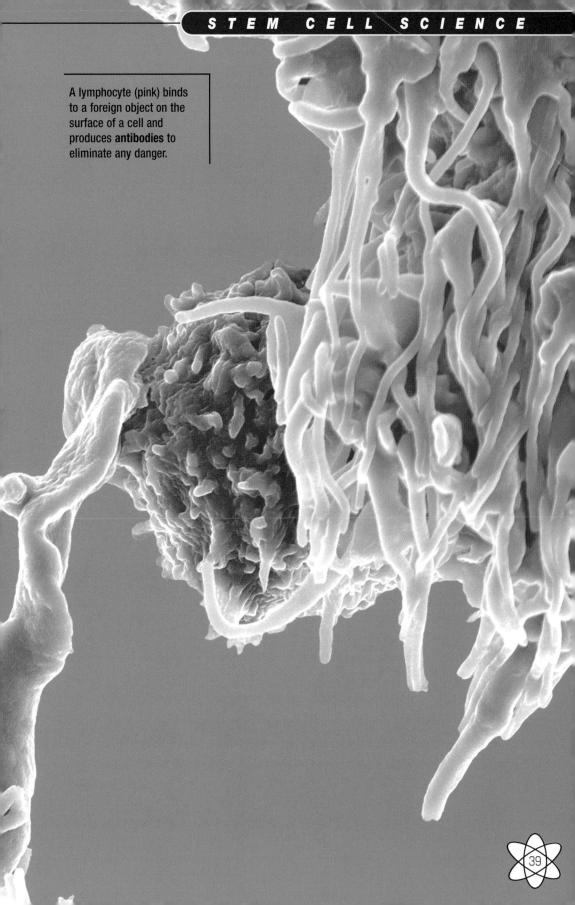

A lymphocyte (pink) binds to a foreign object on the surface of a cell and produces **antibodies** to eliminate any danger.

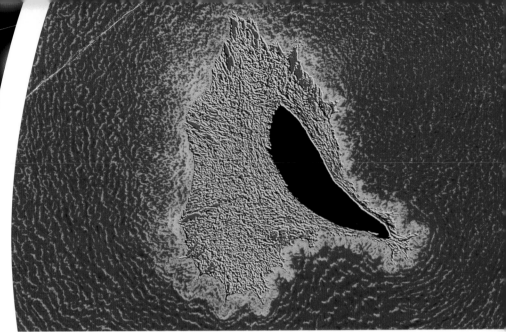

This photograph shows how fatty deposits of plaque (gray) can build up on an artery wall (orange), eventually blocking the artery and possibly causing a heart attack.

BUILDING A NEW HEART

Heart disease is one of the biggest killers in the world, and the number of people affected continues to rise. Experts believe that stem cell treatments in the future could be effective.

Congestive heart failure happens when the heart is not able to pump properly because the cells that usually make it work have become damaged or destroyed. These heart muscle cells are called **cardiomyocytes**, and they may be destroyed by heart attacks, when the supply of blood and oxygen becomes blocked. They can also be damaged by diseases of the arteries or by high blood pressure.

The best way to avoid heart failure is to eat healthily, avoid smoking, and do plenty of exercise. Once the tissues become damaged, the effect is usually irreversible. Drugs that prevent further blockages—clot-busting drugs—can help restore blood flow to the damaged region and prevent further cells from being damaged. However, current research is going one step further in the hope of rebuilding a damaged heart.

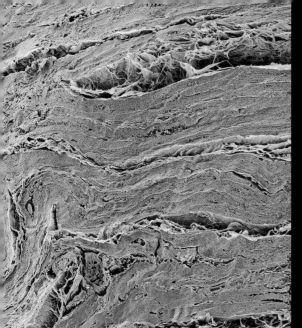

Healthy cardiac muscle (blue) is needed to continuously pump blood around the body.

RECENT STUDIES

So far, experiments have been carried out only on rats and mice, but stem cells have been coaxed into developing into cardiac cells. The stem cells used have been from adult bone marrow in mice and human hematopoeic stem cells.

There have also been studies looking into whether the heart has its own potential stem cells. So far, there is no real evidence of this, although research is still at an early stage. Many millions of stem cells would be needed in order to repair damaged heart tissues. The pace of new discoveries is fast, so it may one day be truly possible to mend a "broken heart."

A CAREER IN SCIENCE

Dr. Steven Houser is the director of the Cardiovascular Research Center (CVRC) at Temple University School of Medicine in Pennsylvania. His laboratory has defined the fundamental mechanisms of cardiac muscle dysfunction that lead to congestive heart failure, the main cause of death in Western society. His work has helped show that the death of cardiac muscle cells brings about heart failure. In 1998, he founded the CVRC to bring investigators together to study the causes and cures of cardiovascular disease.

A DAY IN THE LIFE OF . . .

Dr. Houser's laboratory is currently studying the idea that failing human hearts would have improved function, and patients would live longer, if new cardiac cells could replace the old damaged ones. A typical day involves directing his team in exploring new types of stem cells for cardiac regeneration, evaluating new data, and writing manuscripts and grant proposals to support the science.

THE SCIENTIST SAYS . . .

"I get excited by the potential to learn new things about the human body and use the new information to help people with diseases that reduce the quality and duration of their lives."

As well as the usual in vitro (laboratory) testing for drugs, scientists use computer models to check what effects a medicine is likely to have on patients.

A SAFER WAY OF TESTING

Getting new drugs onto the market is a slow and painstaking process. By the time a new medicine reaches the public, it has been through extensive tests to make sure it is safe and has done what it is supposed to do. Drug companies take great care to ensure the safety of people involved, but this is not always enough.

WHEN DRUG TESTING GOES WRONG

In 2006, six healthy volunteers were given a new drug called TGN1412 that was aimed at treating the inflammatory symptoms of diseases such as rheumatoid arthritis and leukemia. Within seconds of being injected with the drug, the men became seriously ill, some with organ failure. All six have recovered, but they may have long-term health issues that are as yet unknown. Although such an extreme and unexpected response is rare, the Medicines and Healthcare Products Regulatory Agency (MHRA) in the U.K. says that 2,088 volunteers have needed hospital treatment as a result of drug testing since 2001.

When a new drug is developed, it goes through several stages. First, it is tested in a laboratory. Then it is tested on animals, usually

▶▶ http://stemcells.nih.gov/info/scireport/chapter6.asp

rats and mice. Next, it has to be given special clearance to be tested on humans, and if gets this, it is used first on healthy volunteers and then on a select group of patients. Finally, it is tested on a large group of patients. The whole process may take ten years from start to finish.

In the future, stem cell science may speed up this process and protect human volunteers. If human stem cells can be turned into those relevant to a certain drug, they would provide a kind of bridge between animal tests and those carried out on real people. However, this is still many years away.

Patients are carefully vetted by doctors before they test trial drugs.

A CAREER IN SCIENCE

Dr. Gabriel Lasala is the president and scientific director of TCA Cellular Therapy, a research and development company in Louisiana focusing on stem cells. He attended medical school at the National University of Córdoba, Argentina, followed by the Posadas National Hospital in Buenos Aires. After a residency in internal medicine at the same hospital, he went to the University of Mississippi. He founded LifeSource Cryobank, which stores umbilical cord blood and adult stem cells, and the Stem Cell Foundation, which raises funds for stem cell research.

A DAY IN THE LIFE OF . . .

Dr. Lasala runs a daily clinic and performs angioplasties to improve blood flow. He sets aside one or two days each week to perform procedures related to adult stem cell research. These may be bone marrow aspirations to obtain stem cells. In the evenings, he typically does research and writes scientific papers for publication in medical journals.

THE SCIENTIST SAYS . . .

"The most satisfying part of my work is the positive results in patients I am treating with adult stem cells. I hope to achieve effective adult stem cell therapies for cardiovascular diseases."

This technician is examining a tray containing monoclonal antibodies that have been taken from a mouse before inserting it into an automated screening machine.

STEM CELLS AND CANCER

Some stem cells and cancer cells have elements in common, such as the ability to self-renew and make exact copies of themselves. In recent times, scientists have discovered that stem cells and cancer cells share some common genetic features. Stem cell therapy is already being used in cancer treatment via bone marrow transplantation.

Stem cells are used in a variety of ways to help patients produce the blood supply that they need.

TARGETING

Many scientists now think that there may be a very small number—one in a million—of stem cells actually in tumors. These stem cells may be the driving force behind a disease's development. This may open the door for drugs that specifically target these cells, leaving other healthy cells alone.

In trials, a new drug called salinomycin has been shown to target and kill these cells and looks very promising as a future treatment.

Many of the 750 cancer treatments in development around the world are based on stem cell therapies. Researchers are looking at using stem cells as "tumor-seeking vehicles" to chemically confuse cancer cells and cause them to produce toxins. This would, in effect, make them commit suicide. Another stem cell cancer treatment will be tested on human subjects in the near future. This produces **monoclonal antibodies**. Antibodies are proteins in the blood that react to things you are allergic to. Monoclonal antibodies are cloned antibodies that bind to cancer stem cells and disrupt the way in which they work.

This image shows a breast cancer cell (pink) with a molecular model of Herceptin, a drug that blocks cancer growth and kills breast cancer cells.

INVESTIGATING THE EVIDENCE: CANCER CELLS

The investigation: Scientists wanted to establish a systematic method in order to discover drugs to kill cancer stem cells.

The scientists: Dr. Piyush B. Gupta, Broad Institute of MIT and Harvard, Professor Eric S. Lander, MIT and Harvard, Professor Robert A. Weinberg, MIT and Whitehead Institute for Biomedical Research, and Dr. Charlotte Kuperwasser, Tufts University School of Medicine, all of Massachusetts.

Collecting the evidence: The team developed a stable method for growing cancer stem cells in the laboratory. They then treated the cells with 16,000 chemical compounds and looked for those that killed only the cancer stem cells. They used robotic technology to grow the cells in plates that had 384 tiny wells. The robots had arms with 384 tips to add nutrients or chemicals to each well. At the end, the team was able to determine the number of living cells per well and thus identify those compounds that were most effective in killing cancer stem cells.

The conclusion: The team discovered that it is possible to find drugs that selectively kill cancer stem cells. This suggests that future cancer therapies can include anticancer stem cell drugs in combination with traditional drugs so that all of the cancer cells in a tumor can be destroyed.

Most hospitals rely heavily on donated blood to treat all types of conditions, as well as to treat people who have been in accidents, had surgery, or who have given birth.

STEM CELLS AND BLOOD RESEARCH

Maintaining good supplies of donated blood is crucial for hospitals and other health-care facilities. It is less common to use whole blood, so donations are usually separated into blood's different components: plasma, platelets, and red blood cells. Each of these has the potential to be life saving.

Almost one fourth of blood products are used in surgery, and the rest is used across a range of procedures, not only for accidents and emergencies. These include obstetrics, treating blood disorders, and caring for newborn babies. But there are often periods when not enough people are donating blood to keep stocks at an adequare level. The United States and Canada have reported serious drops in supplies in recent times.

ARTIFICIAL BLOOD

There has been a lot of work by a range of scientists toward developing artificial blood, which would be an ideal solution if it could be created in unlimited supplies. One possible source could be from stem cells. In 2005, Luc Douay, a stem cell biologist from the hematological laboratory at the Pierre and Marie Curie University in France, managed to create fully mature human red blood cells from hematopoietic stem cells (see box, right). Scientists in Sweden, France, Australia, and the U.K. are all known to be working on ways to create artificial blood from stem cells. In 2008, a company called Advanced Cell Technology in the U.S. found a way to turn embryonic stem cells into oxygen-carrying red blood cells. The work, however, is still beginning.

The good news is that blood cells do not have a nucleus. This means that they are missing the type of genetic material that can go awry and cause cancer. In theory at least, there should not be a danger from blood made from stem cells. But the work is still at an early stage, and it may still be many years before there is an unlimited supply of artificial blood.

Newborn babies often benefit from the use of blood products that can save their lives.

A CAREER IN SCIENCE

Professor Luc Douay is the group leader of investigations into cell therapies at the Pierre and Marie Curie University in Paris, France. He has been a professor of hematology there since 1991 and the head of the hematological laboratory at the children's hospital Armand Trousseau. He was the medical and scientific director of the French Blood Agency in 1995.

A DAY IN THE LIFE OF . . .

Douay and his team are working on generating red blood cells from stem cells for transfusion medicine. For several years, researchers have been trying to find a substitute for red blood cells. Professor Douay's philosophy is: since we cannot replace nature, we should try to mimic it. A typical day is spent caring for patients in the morning and conducting research in the afternoon. He also drafts publications and grant proposals for further research.

THE SCIENTIST SAYS . . .

"We have sufficient knowledge of the biology of blood stem cells to produce human red blood cells in the laboratory. . . . We have many reasons to think that it will be possible within a few years to produce enough cells to be able to transfuse cultured red blood cells to patients."

CHAPTER SIX

TEETHING TROUBLES

WHEN NEWSPAPER HEADLINES SCREAM THAT A CURE FOR CERTAIN DISEASES IS ON THE CARDS, IT CAN RESULT IN FALSE HOPE FOR THE THOUSANDS OF PEOPLE WHOSE LIVES WOULD BE CHANGED—OR SAVED—BY SUCH A BREAKTHROUGH.

The reality is that the development of new treatments is an extremely slow process. Sometimes, a result that looks very promising in the lab is not borne out when trials begin on humans. There are companies that seek to profit from raised hopes and offer stem cell therapies that have not been tested through proper clinical trials. In the best-case scenario, a patient will lose only his or her money. In the worst case, treatments can endanger lives.

SCIENTIFIC SCANDAL

In 2005, a South Korean scientist, Dr. Hwang Woo-suk, became a national hero when he announced in a paper published in the journal *Science* that he had created the world's first cloned human embryos and had extracted stem cells.

In cloning, embryonic stem cells are extracted and inserted into an egg cell from which the nucleus has been removed.

One year later, the team announced that they had created human embryonic stem cells that were genetically matched to individual patients. But there were question marks over Woo-suk's research, which led the university authorities to investigate. They concluded that the 2004 paper was based on data that had been faked, and the journal retracted both papers. Woo-suk was later charged with accepting $2 million in private donations under false premises, embezzlement, and buying human eggs, which violate South Korean laws. In October 2009, he was convicted and narrowly avoided four years in prison. He received a suspended sentence.

There have also been issues over plagiarism (copying) in a paper that claimed embryonic stem cells were used to create sperm. The scientists concerned are from Newcastle University, U.K., and it transpired that the introduction had been taken from a paper that had not been credited. However, there is no suggestion that the actual science was in question. But when a science is as new as stem cell science, events like these do it no favors.

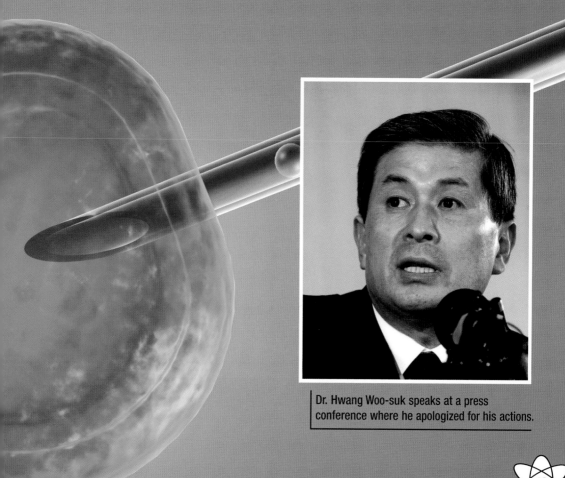

Dr. Hwang Woo-suk speaks at a press conference where he apologized for his actions.

President Barack Obama ended the eight-year-long U.S. stem cell funding ban on February 9, 2009, when he signed a new executive order, fulfilling one of his strongest campaign pledges.

STEM CELLS AND ETHICS

Medical ethics is all about applying morals and judgments to decisions that are taken about medical procedures and research. Stem cell science is not the only branch of medicine where ethics are hotly debated, but it has one of the highest profiles.

STEM CELLS AND POLICY

A lot of the debate revolves around the raw materials required for researching new treatments. Human embryonic stem cells come from embryos that are four or five days old. These are left over from in vitro fertilization (IVF) procedures; only embryos that would have been discarded are used, and there is no way that these embryos could have become babies. However, some people feel very strongly that because an embryo has the potential to become a person, it should not be used in research.

In the United States, until recently there has been a ban on federal funding for research involving embryonic stem cells.

▶▶ http://stemcells.nih.gov/info/ethics.asp

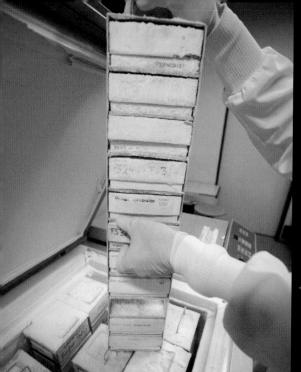

Stem cells have to be preserved in carefully controlled temperatures, here at −112°F (−80°C).

President Barack Obama has reversed this legislation, but some people still object to the idea of embryonic stem cells being used.

The announcement that scientists in Edinburgh, Scotland, led by Sir Ian Wilmut, were able to reprogram skin cells so that they became similar to embryonic stem cells heralds one way in which ethical concerns like these could be addressed. If it were possible to create an unlimited supply of adult stem cells that have the capacity to turn into any cell in the body, the ethical challenges of stem cell science would be old news.

A CAREER IN SCIENCE

Dr. Tenneille Ludwig is a senior scientist at WiCell Research Institute, a nonprofit research organization established to support human embryonic stem cell research at the University of Wisconsin-Madison and worldwide. Dr. Ludwig developed the first defined system to sustain and nourish human embryonic stem cells using a nutrient called TeSR1. Her work now focuses on improving stem cell cultures.

A DAY IN THE LIFE . . .

Dr. Ludwig oversees a research laboratory, so most of her time is spent designing experiments and analyzing the results, while others perform the experiments. A portion of her job involves meeting and exchanging information with other scientists. She believes the harder you work and the better the results you produce, the more opportunities you have to both share your experiences and learn from the experiences of others.

THE SCIENTIST SAYS . . .

"The most satisfying part for me is the experience of investigating problems and looking for solutions. There is a point at which you arrive at an answer. For a brief moment in time, you are the only one in the world who knows what you know. You then have the opportunity to share that knowledge with the rest of the world—and that leads to more questions and more solutions."

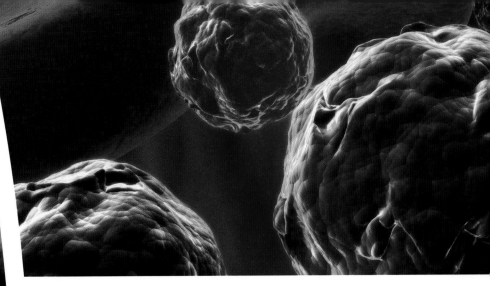

Lymphocytes, a type of white blood cell, are the human body's natural immune response to attacks from viruses (above), bacteria, and other invaders.

THE PROBLEMS OF TISSUE REJECTION

Our immune system is constantly working to fight off invaders in the form of microbes, viruses, and other harmful substances. But when someone receives a transplant of tissue or organs (or even blood, if it is not the correct match), the body may see this as an invader and set off a chain of aggressive and harmful responses.

A person in this situation—for example, someone who has had a kidney transplant—will be given immunosuppressants to restrain the effects of the immune response. This can leave the patient open to all types of other infections, and he or she may have to take the drugs for the rest of their lives. The only exceptions to this are transplants of the cornea in the eye, which has no blood supply. This means the immune system's "soldiers," or antibodies, cannot reach the area through the bloodstream. Transplants between identical twins are also usually an exception because their tissue types are likely to be similar.

ALTERNATIVE TREATMENTS

Treatments based on stem cells may lead to tissue rejection if the stem cells come from a different person. The only ways to avoid this is if the cells come from the patients themselves or if the stem cells

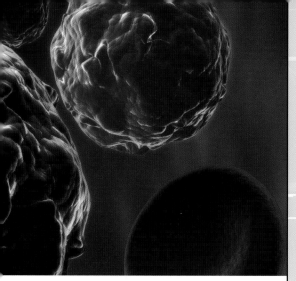

are engineered in such a way that they can deal with this immune response. One promising approach is the use of embryonic stem cells in which the DNA has been replaced with the patient's own DNA. This is called therapeutic cloning, but it is not the same as reproductive cloning. There is no creation of copied human beings or fertilization involved.

Another approach would be to destroy a patient's own immune system and replace it with immune cells from a donor. But this is a very risky procedure and leaves the patient open to infection for many months while the new immune system starts working. Finding a way to use stem cells so that they are not rejected as foreign tissue remains one of the biggest challenges in this field, and many scientists around the world are working on this.

INVESTIGATING THE EVIDENCE: NEW SOURCES OF STEM CELLS

The investigation: Scientists wanted to create a new source of pluripotent stem cells without the use or destruction of embryos. This could include the development of the world's first universal stem cell bank and the potential for treatment of large populations without a need for immunosuppressives or the risk of tissue rejection.

The scientists: Dr. Elena Revazova and Dr. Nikolay Turovets from International Stem Cell Corporation (ISCO), a company in California.

Collecting the evidence: Ooycytes are unfertilized egg cells. The team retrieved mature oocytes from women following normal or induced ovulation. Using chemicals to mimic aspects of what a sperm does, they showed that the resulting stem cells were pluripotent.

The conclusion: ISCO has created stem cells from female egg donors and transformed these into cells with different characteristics. This may enable regenerative medical treatment without immunosuppression.

THE DANGERS OF CELLULAR OVERDRIVE

Cancer is essentially what happens when cells start to change and grow in an uncontrolled manner. Normal cells have certain characteristics—for example, they make exact copies of themselves, they stop reproducing at the right time, they stick together in the correct way, they self-destruct if they are damaged, and they become specialized, which means that they perform specific functions. Cancer cells, on the other hand, do not stop reproducing, do not obey signals from other cells, do not stick together, and do not specialize.

NORMAL CELLS VERSUS CANCER CELLS

In 2009, there were several major breakthroughs in this area of research. Two separate teams, at the University of Edinburgh, Scotland, and Mount Sinai Hospital in Toronto, Canada, announced separately that they had found a way to insert raw DNA into a cell and then remove the DNA once the genes had worked as they needed them to. The genetic link with cancer is that a type of gene called an oncogene is one that causes normal cells to transform into cancerous ones.

But that is not the only connection between stem cells and cancer.

This light micrograph shows a microinjection of a single cell, introducing foreign DNA into the nucleus, a technique that is used in cancer research.

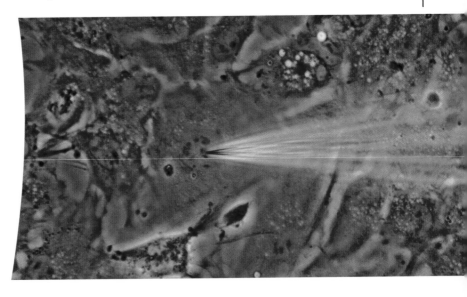

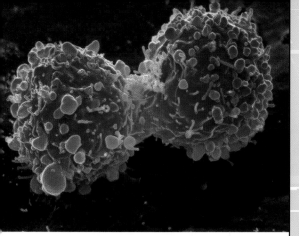

This is a lung cancer cell dividing to produce two daughter cells. Cancer cells divide very quickly in a chaotic, uncontrolled manner.

INVESTIGATING THE EVIDENCE: FISH STUDY

The investigation: The zebra fish is useful for studying cancer and stem cells because its genes are very similar to those of humans. A team decided to grow a zebra fish that was transparent as an adult so that they could see every detail of stem and cancer cell behavior inside of it.

The scientists: Dr. Richard White of the Dana-Farber Cancer Institute and Harvard Medical School, Jennifer Cech of Children's Hospital Boston, Anna Sessa of the University of Texas at Austin, Chris Burke of the University of Massachusetts, and Frank Chen of Harvard University. The team also included Leonard Zon of Children's Hospital Boston.

Collecting the evidence: The team isolated donor stem cells from an animal in which the stem cells were marked with green fluorescent protein (GFP) and transplanted them into a zebra fish. The cells took three weeks of moving around the blood until they anchored themselves into the bone marrow. The team calculated this by figuring out how much GFP there was in the bone marrow. They then did the same thing with the cancer cells.

The conclusion: The information has now been shared with 100 labs around the world. The team discovered that the way in which these cells find their home is dynamic and organized.

CHAPTER SEVEN

GENE THERAPY AND STEM CELLS

GENE THERAPY AND THE THERAPEUTIC USE OF STEM CELLS ARE NEW AND EXPERIMENTAL BRANCHES OF SCIENCE THAT HAVE ENORMOUS POTENTIAL. THERE ARE AROUND 450 GENE THERAPY TRIALS UNDER WAY IN THE UNITED STATES ALONE. A SIGNIFICANT NUMBER OF THESE INVOLVE STEM CELLS.

WHAT IS GENE THERAPY?

Gene therapy is the process of replacing abnormal genes, which cause disease, with genes that are healthy. Getting the genes to the correct place is extremely difficult, and viruses are often used as the carrier. Viruses have a fundamental property that makes them ideal for this role. They infect healthy cells by placing their own genetic material inside a cell as they do so. Scientists have found that, by manipulating them in the right way, they can also be made to deliver a healthy gene into a damaged cell.

Stem cells are potentially useful for gene therapy because they have the ability to self-renew. In theory, this means a treatment based on gene therapy would not have to be repeatedly administered in order to keep a patient healthy. The stem cells would simply keep making healthy copies that would specialize and would always be missing the damaged gene.

There is a lot to be excited about in this field, but one of the first researchers into gene therapy, James Wilson of Philadelphia University in Pennsylvania, has highlighted a gene therapy study that resulted in the death of an 18-year-old man in 1999. He warned scientists that they should be careful about the hype surrounding gene therapy.

By using the hereditary information encoded in people's DNA (right), it may be possible to cure hereditary diseases in the future.

This corneal strip has been grown in a laboratory. It comes from the cells that line the cornea and, in the right conditions, can be used in the treatment of eye disorders.

TISSUE ENGINEERING

Transplant surgery has been around for more than 50 years. But there are never enough organs to go around, and when organs are available, there are always problems with the rejection of foreign tissue. So what if there were an unlimited supply of organs grown from a patient's cells, with no compatibility issues?

This is one of the goals of tissue engineering, which is the science of manipulating cells into making new tissues. This may be anything from cartilage to skin, muscles, or bone— or even entire organs, such as a heart, kidney, or liver.

CELLS AND SCAFFOLDS

Getting new tissues to grow must begin with individual cells. They need to be grown on what is known as a scaffold, a structure that will help them form the right shape and properties. They also act as life-support systems and must have a plentiful supply of blood and other substances that they need in order to thrive. The cells may be a combination of the patient's and those of donors.

Various materials may be used as scaffolds in tissue engineering, including silicon chips and collagen. Collagen is a protein found in large quantities in the human body. It is referred to as the "glue" that

▶▶ http://learn.genetics.utah.edu/content/tech/stemcells/scfuture

This block of tissue scaffold will be seeded with live human cells to create bioartificial tissue.

holds our organs and skin together. In tissue engineering, all tissue cells may be stripped away and replaced with new cells. Once the tissue has grown enough to sustain itself, the collagen scaffold dissolves.

As stem cell science is also about finding ways to help the body regenerate and create new healthy cells instead of diseased ones, it has a promising place in the science of tissue engineering. In 2008, a woman in Spain received a new trachea, or windpipe, in an operation that saved her life. The trachea had been grown from her own cells, including stem cells. It was grown on a scaffold made from a small piece of the windpipe of a patient who had died and donated it. The operation was a complete success.

INVESTIGATING THE EVIDENCE: TRACKING CELL LINES

The investigation: The goal was to genetically modify a human embryonic stem cell line so that a fluorescent protein could be used to track the development of red blood cells from human embryonic stem cells.

The scientists: Professors Andrew Elefanty and Ed Stanley of the Immunology and Stem Cell Laboratories, Monash University, Victoria, Australia, and their team.

Collecting the evidence: The team inserted DNA coded for a green fluorescent jellyfish protein (GFP) to make the cells fluoresce green under light of a certain wavelength. They then inserted DNA encoding for a red fluorescent protein (RFP) into the cells so that only developing red blood cells would fluoresce red.

The conclusion: The team showed that the cells glowed green with GFP but that only red blood cells fluoresced red with RFP. Only the red fluorescing cells had turned on the genes for human hemoglobin. When the team transplanted the cells into mice, they were able to identify the human cells by their red and green fluorescence.

STEM CELLS—A WORLD OF POSSIBILITY

When U.S. President Barack Obama removed the ban on funding for stem cell research in 2009, it gave a huge boost to scientists working on stem cells worldwide. Researchers benefit from advancements and leaps in knowledge even when they are not part of the team that has made them. New techniques and breakthroughs filter into the scientific community and help drive forward research.

In December 2009, the U.S. National Institutes of Health authorized 13 embryonic stem cell lines—11 by Children's Hospital Boston, Massachusetts, and two by Rockefeller University in New York City—for study by scientists using public funds.

EARLY DAYS

Stem cell science is still at an early stage of development, and the dream of replacing worn or diseased cells with those that function normally is still many years away in most cases. There are huge technical hurdles to be cleared, and some people are strongly against these developments on ethical and religious grounds.

A search under the term "stem cells" in Google News brought up around 4,000 stories that had been in the press over the preceding ten days. Stem cells are a hot topic and one that will continue to generate fervent debate, some of it heated. However, the research brings hope to the many people whose lives have been changed by accidents or diseases.

Unfortunately, the day when treatments are easily available may still involve a long wait. In September 2009, an investigation by a newspaper in the U.K. found that hundreds of desperate parents had spent up to £30,000 ($45,000) each on unproven stem cell treatments on offer in China to treat their children's conditions. One leading scientist described the risk level of seeking these treatments as being on a par with child abuse. It is understandable that people facing long-term or terminal illnesses will grasp at straws, but these stories should not detract from the real progress that is being made in stem cell research.

Now that restrictions have been lifted on research in the United States, the future does truly look bright for stem cell science.

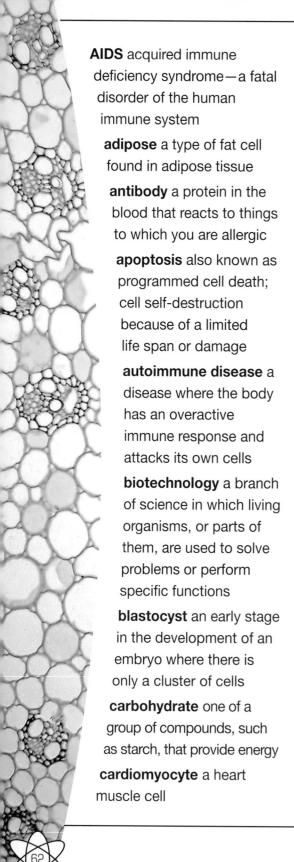

AIDS acquired immune deficiency syndrome—a fatal disorder of the human immune system

adipose a type of fat cell found in adipose tissue

antibody a protein in the blood that reacts to things to which you are allergic

apoptosis also known as programmed cell death; cell self-destruction because of a limited life span or damage

autoimmune disease a disease where the body has an overactive immune response and attacks its own cells

biotechnology a branch of science in which living organisms, or parts of them, are used to solve problems or perform specific functions

blastocyst an early stage in the development of an embryo where there is only a cluster of cells

carbohydrate one of a group of compounds, such as starch, that provide energy

cardiomyocyte a heart muscle cell

cell line cells grown in a tissue culture that are the product of a single parent group of cells

cloning the process of producing a living system that is genetically identical to its ancestor

DNA deoxyribonucleic acid—the chemical from which our genetic "blueprint' is made

embryo an organism in the early stages of development in the womb

embryonic stem cell a stem cell derived from the inner cell mass (ICM) of a human embryo before it has specialized

enzyme a biological catalyst that speeds up chemical reactions occurring in the bodies of living things

eukaryotic describes organisms that have more than one cell

gene a portion of a molecule of DNA that controls the characteristics that an offspring will inherit

gene therapy genetic engineering to replace abnormal genes that cause disease with genes that are healthy

hematopoietic describes a multipotent stem cell that gives rise to all types of blood cells

hemorrhagic stroke a type of stroke caused by a blood vessel bursting in the brain

induced pluripotent stem (iPS) cell an adult cell that has been genetically reprogrammed so that it can become any type of cell

inner cell mass (ICM) the inner part of a blastocyst containing the cells that will make up the human body

insulin a hormone that regulates glucose (blood sugar) in the body

ischemic stroke a type of stroke caused by a blood clot, or a bleed

lymph a fluid that travels through the body carrying cells that help fight infection and disease

lymphocyte a type of white blood cell that plays an important role in the body's defenses

mitochondrion a structure that provides energy for a cell (plural: mitochondria)

monoclonal antibody a cloned antibody that binds to cancer stem cells and disrupts the way in which they work

multipotent having the ability to give rise to many but specialized types of cells

neuron a nerve cell; a cell of the brain and nervous system

nucleus the structure that contains a cell's hereditary information and controls its growth and reproduction

organelle a structure within a cell that performs a specific function

pancreatic islet cell also called islet of Langerhans; a region of the pancreas that produces hormones such as insulin

plasma membrane a cell's outer membrane that separates and protects it from anything exterior

pluripotent describes cells that have the ability to become any of the types of cells in the body

prokaryotic describes single-celled organisms that cannot develop or change into more complex forms

ribosome a part of a cell that produces the cell's proteins

therapeutic concerned with the treatment of disease

totipotent describes a cell that has the capacity to become a complete organism or a cell that will specialize into pluripotent cells

trophoblast the outermost layer of cells of a blastocyst, which develops into part of the placenta

zygote a fertilized cell